The Galaxy S24 Ultra Chronicles

*An Insider's Must-Read Guide Before You
Upgrade (Untold Features)*

Tech Talker

Table of contents

Introduction

In the ever-evolving landscape of smartphones, the Samsung Galaxy S24 Ultra emerges as a beacon of innovation and sophistication. Unveiled to the world on January 17, 2024, and swiftly making its way to the market on January 31, this device transcends the ordinary, promising a smartphone experience like no other.

What sets the Galaxy S24 Ultra apart is not just its impressive design or the expected hardware upgrades; it's the allure of being an insider privy to untold features that truly makes this smartphone a compelling choice. As we embark on this journey through the Galaxy S24 Ultra Chronicles, we'll unravel the significance of being in the know, exploring features that transcend the ordinary and redefine the boundaries of what a smartphone can achieve. This isn't just a phone; it's an insider's guide to the future of smartphone technology. Join me as we uncover the secrets that make the Samsung Galaxy S24 Ultra a revolutionary device, offering an exclusive glimpse into the untold features that await those seeking the pinnacle of mobile innovation. The Insider's Must-Read Guide Before You Upgrade is your key to unlocking the full potential of this extraordinary device.

Chapter 1:
Unveiling the Marvel

1.1 The Grand Revelation

As of today, January 19, 2024, the tech world is still buzzing with excitement after Samsung's revelation on January 17, 2024, of the groundbreaking Galaxy S24 Ultra. This wasn't just another smartphone announcement; it was a glimpse into the future of mobile technology.

On this groundbreaking day, Samsung set the stage for a new era in smartphones. The announcement of the Galaxy S24 Ultra wasn't merely about showcasing a device; it was a declaration of innovation, a testament to the relentless pursuit of perfection in the world of technology. Tech enthusiasts, industry experts, and smartphone aficionados around the globe tuned in to witness the unveiling of a device that promised to redefine their expectations.

The announcement date wasn't just about revealing specifications and features; it was an immersive experience, a virtual journey into the capabilities of a device designed to surpass its predecessors. The tech community held its breath as the curtain was lifted, marking the beginning of a new chapter in the smartphone saga.

Just two weeks after the grand revelation, on January 31, 2024, the Galaxy S24 Ultra is set to make its official debut in the market. The significance of this date lies in the transformation of a concept into a tangible reality for consumers worldwide. It isn't just a release; it's the birth of a technological revolution.

The market release of the Galaxy S24 Ultra means that users can now hold in their hands a device that has garnered admiration and curiosity during its announcement. It marks the moment when the smartphone ceases to be a mere topic of speculation and becomes an accessible marvel for those eager to embrace cutting-edge technology.

In the weeks and days preceding the grand announcement of the Galaxy S24 Ultra on January 17, 2024, the tech community was alive with fervent anticipation. Samsung had successfully woven a web of excitement, leaving enthusiasts and critics alike eager to witness the unveiling of the next big thing in the world of smartphones.

As with any highly anticipated device, the rumor mill had been churning at full throttle. Leaked specifications, speculative features, and tantalizing teasers had set the stage for a device that promised to transcend the boundaries of conventional smartphones. The anticipation was not merely about another iteration of a flagship; it was about the promise of innovation, the allure of the unknown.

Tech forums and social media platforms were ablaze with discussions and debates. Enthusiasts dissected every leaked image, analyzed purported features, and speculated on how the Galaxy S24 Ultra would shape the future of mobile technology. Samsung's strategic release of teasers only fueled the anticipation, providing glimpses into a device shrouded in secrecy, heightening the collective curiosity of the tech-savvy audience.

What intensified the anticipation wasn't just the anticipation of confirmed specifications but the hunger for the untold features – the surprises that Samsung had managed to keep under wraps. The prospect of being an insider, privy to features not yet revealed to the public, added an extra layer of excitement.

As we approached the fateful day of January 17, 2024, the anticipation reached a crescendo. The tech world stood on the brink of a new era, awaiting the revelation of a device that would not only meet expectations but shatter them, leaving an indelible mark on the landscape of smartphones.

1.2 Design Elegance

When it comes to flagship smartphones, design isn't just a visual aspect – it's a statement. With the Galaxy S24 Ultra, Samsung set out not only to create a device of unparalleled functionality but also to elevate the very essence of aesthetic appeal.

The first glance at the Galaxy S24 Ultra reveals a device that epitomizes sleekness. Samsung's design team has meticulously refined the smartphone's silhouette, giving it a slimmer profile without compromising on its substantial screen real estate. The bezels, now even more minimalistic, seamlessly merge with the display, offering an immersive visual experience.

Beyond dimensions, the choice of materials plays a pivotal role in the device's overall appeal. The Galaxy S24 Ultra doesn't just use premium materials; it redefines them. The incorporation of cutting-edge alloys and resilient glass not only enhances durability but also contributes to a device that feels inherently premium in the palm of your hand.

Samsung has always been known for pushing the boundaries of color in smartphone design. The Galaxy S24 Ultra continues this tradition with an innovative color palette that goes beyond the ordinary. From subtle gradients that shift dynamically in the light to bold, eye-catching hues, the device isn't just a phone; it's a piece of art that reflects the user's personality.

Design isn't just about appearances; it's about how a device feels in your hands. The Galaxy S24 Ultra excels in ergonomic design, with every curve and contour meticulously crafted for a comfortable grip. The placement of buttons, the accessibility of features, and the intuitive user interface contribute to an overall user experience that transcends mere functionality.

Galaxy S24 Ultra vs. Its Predecessors

As technology advances, each iteration of a flagship smartphone seeks to outshine its predecessor. The Galaxy S24 Ultra, in its pursuit of excellence, brings forth notable changes from the S23 Ultra and a remarkable evolution from the S22 Ultra.

One of the standout features of the Galaxy S24 Ultra lies in its camera system. Building upon the already stellar capabilities of the S23 Ultra, Samsung has introduced groundbreaking advancements that redefine mobile photography. The increased sensor sizes, enhanced low-light performance, and artificial intelligence-driven optimizations mark a significant leap forward.

While the S23 Ultra boasted impressive processing capabilities, the Galaxy S24 Ultra takes it a step further. The latest processor, coupled with increased RAM and storage options, ensures seamless multitasking, faster app launches, and a more responsive overall user experience. Whether you're a power user or a casual smartphone enthusiast, the improvements are impossible to ignore.

In the realm of battery life, the Galaxy S24 Ultra aims not just to meet expectations but to exceed them. With enhanced battery optimization algorithms and more efficient hardware, users can expect a device that lasts longer on a single charge. Moreover, the charging speed has seen a substantial boost, ensuring that you spend less time plugged in and more time enjoying your device.

The S22 Ultra set a high bar for display quality, but the S24 Ultra elevates it further. The new display technology not only enhances visual clarity and brightness but also introduces innovative features that adapt to different lighting conditions. Whether you're indoors, outdoors, or somewhere in between, the Galaxy S24 Ultra's display is designed to deliver an unparalleled viewing experience.

Chapter 2:

Titanium Transformation

2.1 Strength in Material

In the ever-evolving landscape of smartphone materials, the Galaxy S24 Ultra takes a bold step by bidding farewell to aluminum and embracing the durability of titanium. This switch in the phone's frame material is not just a design choice; it's a statement about resilience and a commitment to delivering a device that stands the test of time.

Titanium, known for its exceptional strength-to-weight ratio and resistance to corrosion, brings a new level of robustness to the Galaxy S24 Ultra. The frame, crafted from this aerospace-grade material, not only adds a touch of sophistication but also ensures that the device can endure the rigors of daily use without succumbing to wear and tear.

Despite its formidable strength, titanium is surprisingly lightweight. This translates into a smartphone that doesn't compromise on durability while maintaining a comfortable and manageable weight. The Galaxy S24 Ultra, with its titanium frame, strikes a harmonious balance between strength and practicality, offering users a device that feels substantial in hand without being cumbersome.

The transition from aluminum to titanium is not merely a superficial change. It signifies an enhancement in structural integrity, providing additional protection to internal components. This is particularly crucial in the context of accidental drops or impacts, where the frame plays a pivotal role in safeguarding the device's internal circuitry.

Beyond its mechanical properties, titanium imparts a sleek and premium aesthetic to the Galaxy S24 Ultra. The frame's finish not only exudes elegance but also resists fingerprints and scratches, contributing to the overall pristine look of the device.

The advantages of titanium

Titanium, a material synonymous with strength and resilience, emerges as the hero in the Galaxy S24 Ultra's structural narrative. This aerospace-grade alloy brings forth a trifecta of advantages—strength, heat conduction, and weight—that collectively elevate the smartphone experience to new heights.

1. Strength Beyond Measure

Titanium's reputation as an exceptionally robust material is grounded in its superior strength-to-weight ratio. In the Galaxy S24 Ultra, this translates into a device that not only withstands the trials of everyday use but also emerges unscathed from unexpected mishaps. The structural integrity provided by titanium ensures that the smartphone remains a stalwart companion, resilient against the knocks and bumps of modern life.

2. Heat Conduction Excellence

Efficient heat conduction is pivotal for maintaining optimal performance, especially in high-powered devices like the Galaxy S24 Ultra. Titanium's natural ability to dissipate heat ensures that the phone stays cool even during resource-intensive tasks. This not only contributes to sustained performance but also enhances the longevity of internal components, providing users with a device that excels in both power and durability.

3. Weightless Might

While titanium is renowned for its strength, it doesn't burden the Galaxy S24 Ultra with unnecessary heft. The lightweight nature of titanium ensures that users enjoy a device that feels substantial in hand without compromising on comfort. The smartphone becomes a companion that seamlessly integrates into daily life, effortlessly blending durability with a feather-light touch.

2.2 Flatter and Fresher

In a departure from its curved predecessors, the Galaxy S24 Ultra introduces a bold shift to a flat display, marking a significant evolution in Samsung's design philosophy. This departure from the curved edges is not merely a stylistic choice but a strategic move that ushers in a new era of user experience and aesthetic appeal.

1. Practicality Meets Aesthetics

The decision to embrace a flat display is rooted in the pursuit of practicality and user-centric design. While curved screens indeed contributed to a futuristic aesthetic in previous models, the flat display in the Galaxy S24 Ultra prioritizes functionality without compromising on visual elegance.

Users can now enjoy a display that not only offers a more natural grip but also minimizes accidental touches along the edges, enhancing the overall usability of the device.

2. Enhanced Durability and Protection

A flat display brings with it a robustness that goes beyond aesthetics. The S24 Ultra's screen, unencumbered by curved edges, becomes inherently more durable and less prone to accidental damage. The absence of exposed curved edges reduces the vulnerability of the display, offering users a sense of security and peace of mind as they navigate their digital realms.

3. Aesthetic Simplicity and Immersive Content

The flat display, with its clean and uncomplicated design, serves as an unobtrusive canvas for the content users engage with daily. Whether viewing multimedia, playing games, or scrolling through social media, the flat screen maximizes the immersive experience by eliminating distractions. This design choice aligns with Samsung's commitment to delivering an unfiltered, immersive visual experience that places content at the forefront.

As we embrace this shift to a flat display in the Galaxy S24 Ultra, it becomes evident that Samsung's design decisions are not arbitrary but purposeful, driven by a desire to enhance user experience and redefine the standards of smartphone aesthetics.

The benefits of flat screens and the quest for symmetry

The flat screen of the Galaxy S24 Ultra brings forth a wave of practicality, redefining how users engage with their smartphones. One standout benefit is the enhancement of multitasking capabilities. The absence of curved edges means that users can seamlessly navigate between applications without the fear of accidental touches interfering with their workflow. This results in a more efficient and frustration-free multitasking experience, a testament to the user-centric design philosophy behind the Galaxy S24 Ultra.

The quest for symmetry has been a driving force in the transition to a flat display. Samsung's commitment to delivering a harmonious and balanced design is evident in the Galaxy S24 Ultra. The flat screen contributes to a clean and symmetrical appearance, accentuating the device's overall aesthetic appeal. This pursuit of symmetry is not merely a visual choice but a deliberate effort to create a device that feels balanced and comfortable in the hands of the user.

The flat display extends its influence to the immersive nature of content consumption. With a screen that seamlessly stretches from edge to edge, users can enjoy a more immersive viewing experience. Whether watching videos, playing games, or simply scrolling through content, the flat screen eliminates visual distractions, allowing users to focus entirely on the captivating content before them.

Beyond aesthetics, the flat screen contributes to the device's durability. The absence of curved edges reduces vulnerability to accidental drops, offering users a device that not only looks sleek but also stands up to the rigors of daily use. The flat design, therefore, represents a harmonious union of aesthetics and practicality, embodying Samsung's commitment to delivering a device that not only looks good but also performs reliably.

In the pursuit of a seamless, balanced, and immersive user experience, the Galaxy S24 Ultra's transition to a flat display is more than just a design choice; it's a step toward redefining the standards of functionality and aesthetics in the world of smartphones.

2.3 Matte Magic

In the grand symphony of design, the Galaxy S24 Ultra introduces a captivating element – the matte finish. This subtle yet sophisticated texture not only adds a touch of elegance to the device but also serves a practical purpose. The matte finish minimizes fingerprint smudges, ensuring that the phone retains its pristine appearance even after prolonged use. It's a testament to Samsung's commitment to marrying aesthetics with user-centric functionality.

The devil, they say, is in the details, and the textured side rails of the Galaxy S24 Ultra are a testament to the meticulous attention Samsung pays to every aspect of the user experience. Running your fingers along these finely textured rails provides a sensory delight, offering a secure and comfortable grip. This not only adds a tactile dimension to the device but also enhances the overall handling experience, ensuring that the Galaxy S24 Ultra feels like a natural extension of the user's hand.

Color is an expressive language, and the Galaxy S24 Ultra speaks it fluently with its array of dazzling color options. From subtle sophistication to bold statements, users can choose a hue that resonates with their personal style. The new color palette not only adds vibrancy to the device but also allows users to make a statement with their choice. Samsung's commitment to providing a diverse range of options ensures that there's a Galaxy S24 Ultra for every taste and preference.

As you delve into the Galaxy S24 Ultra, take a moment to appreciate the mastery of the matte finish, savor the tactile pleasure of the textured side rails, and explore the vibrant spectrum of color options. Samsung's dedication to both form and function shines through, creating a device that is not just a tool but a work of art that you can carry in your pocket.

The Subtle Color Changes and comparisons to iPhone 15 Pro

In the realm of smartphone design, nuances matter, and the Galaxy S24 Ultra embraces this philosophy with its subtle yet impactful color changes. Samsung has orchestrated a chromatic ballet, introducing nuanced shifts in color tones that elevate the visual appeal of the device. These subtle changes are not just about aesthetics; they reflect Samsung's dedication to creating an immersive and visually pleasing user experience.

As we traverse the landscape of premium smartphones, comparisons are inevitable. The Galaxy S24 Ultra finds itself on the same stage as the iPhone 15 Pro, inviting users to evaluate and appreciate the distinctive characteristics of each device. While both phones boast cutting-edge technology and design prowess, the Galaxy S24 Ultra sets itself apart with its unique color palette. The subtle color changes in the Galaxy S24 Ultra add a layer of sophistication, providing users with a device that not only performs exceptionally but also captivates the eyes with its refined aesthetics.

While the iPhone 15 Pro may be a formidable competitor, the Galaxy S24 Ultra's subtle color changes serve as a testament to Samsung's commitment to continuous refinement. It's not just about appearances; it's about creating a holistic experience where aesthetics seamlessly blend with functionality. As users explore the Galaxy S24 Ultra's color variations, they embark on a journey into the heart of Samsung's design philosophy – where every detail, no matter how subtle, contributes to the overall brilliance of the device.

Chapter 3:

Hardware Horizon

3.1 RAM Boost

In the relentless pursuit of elevating user experience, Samsung has endowed the Galaxy S24 Ultra with a significant boost in RAM, transcending from 8GB in its predecessor to a formidable 12GB. This upgrade is not merely a numerical progression; it is a strategic enhancement that amplifies the device's overall performance, promising users a seamless and responsive interaction with their smartphones.

With the expanded 12GB RAM, the Galaxy S24 Ultra transforms into a multitasking powerhouse. Users can seamlessly switch between applications, run resource-intensive processes, and indulge in graphics-heavy gaming without encountering the dreaded lag. This upgrade is a testament to Samsung's commitment to providing users with a device that effortlessly keeps pace with the demands of modern digital lifestyles.

As technology hurtles into the future, the need for robust hardware becomes paramount. The Galaxy S24 Ultra's RAM upgrade is a forward-looking move, ensuring that users are well-equipped to navigate the evolving landscape of mobile applications and services. Whether it's juggling multiple apps, editing high-resolution videos, or engaging in augmented reality experiences, the 12GB RAM stands as a guardian of smooth and efficient performance.

In the realm of smartphones, performance is not just a specification; it's the cornerstone of user satisfaction. The Galaxy S24 Ultra's enhanced RAM capacity is poised to elevate the user experience, providing a device that doesn't just meet expectations but surpasses them. From lightning-fast app launches to fluid navigation through the device's interface, every interaction with the Galaxy S24 Ultra becomes a testament to the harmonious synergy between hardware and user-centric design.

As users embrace the Galaxy S24 Ultra, they welcome not just a device with increased RAM but a gateway to a new echelon of mobile performance – an echelon where speed, responsiveness, and multitasking prowess converge to redefine the standards of smartphone excellence.

In the ever-evolving landscape of smartphone technology, the "Ultra" moniker isn't just a label; it's a promise of uncompromised excellence. The Galaxy S24 Ultra not only lives up to this promise but propels it to new heights through its unparalleled performance upgrades. Let's delve into the significance of these improvements, understanding how they elevate the Ultra phone experience to unprecedented levels.

An Ultra phone isn't just about making calls and sending messages; it's a comprehensive tool that caters to the diverse and demanding needs of its users. With improved performance, the Galaxy S24 Ultra effortlessly tackles resource-intensive tasks. From high-definition video editing to seamless multitasking across a myriad of applications, users can delve into a realm of possibilities, unencumbered by performance constraints.

For gaming enthusiasts, an Ultra phone is the gateway to a world of immersive experiences. The enhanced performance of the Galaxy S24 Ultra translates to smoother frame rates, faster load times, and a level of responsiveness that can make the difference between victory and defeat in competitive gaming scenarios. The device's improved RAM becomes the secret weapon, ensuring that every gaming session is not just enjoyable but a showcase of cutting-edge mobile gaming capabilities.

The Galaxy S24 Ultra isn't just a device for today; it's a companion for the future. As technology advances and applications become more sophisticated, the improved performance of the Ultra phone stands as a beacon of readiness. Users can confidently embrace the ever-expanding landscape of mobile technology, knowing that their device is equipped to handle the challenges and opportunities that tomorrow may bring.

Beyond the technical specifications, the significance of improved performance resonates in the day-to-day experiences of users. The Galaxy S24 Ultra isn't just a smartphone; it's an extension of one's digital identity. The enhanced performance ensures that every interaction, from opening apps to navigating through the device's interface, is a seamless and delightful experience. The Ultra phone isn't just about meeting expectations; it's about exceeding them, making every moment with the device a testament to Samsung's commitment to excellence.

In essence, the improved performance of the Galaxy S24 Ultra isn't a mere feature; it's a transformative force that redefines what users can expect from an Ultra phone. As users embark on a journey with the Galaxy S24 Ultra, they enter a realm where performance isn't just a specification but a cornerstone of an extraordinary smartphone experience.

3.2 Sonic Upgrade

In the pursuit of crafting the ultimate smartphone experience, Samsung has left no stone unturned, and this commitment extends to the auditory realm. The internal speaker design of the Galaxy S24 Ultra undergoes a transformative evolution, promising users an enhanced audio experience that transcends the ordinary.

The internal speaker design of the Galaxy S24 Ultra is a testament to the marriage of art and science. Samsung engineers, with an unwavering dedication to perfection, have meticulously fine-tuned the acoustic components to achieve a level of precision that elevates the audio quality to new heights. Whether it's the subtle nuances of a melody or the thunderous beats of a bass-heavy track, every note is delivered with utmost clarity and fidelity.

Step into a world where audio isn't just heard; it's experienced. The enhanced internal speaker design creates a sense of immersive surround sound that captivates the listener. Whether you're engrossed in a gripping movie, indulging in your favorite music, or navigating the dynamic soundscape of a game, the Galaxy S24 Ultra transforms your smartphone into a portable entertainment hub, delivering an audio experience that transcends expectations.

The Galaxy S24 Ultra isn't just about volume; it's about the delicate dance between dynamic range and clarity. The internal speaker design strikes a harmonious balance, ensuring that every audio nuance is preserved. From the gentlest whisper to the most thunderous crescendo, users can savor the full spectrum of sound with a level of detail that redefines what's possible in a smartphone.

Recognizing that every user has unique preferences, the Galaxy S24 Ultra introduces adaptive audio enhancement. This innovative feature tailors the audio output based on the content being consumed and the user's individual preferences. Whether you're in the mood for a bass-heavy experience or a more balanced audio profile, the Galaxy S24 Ultra adapts, ensuring that your auditory journey is precisely as you desire.

In essence, the changes in the internal speaker design of the Galaxy S24 Ultra are not merely technical upgrades; they are a symphony of innovation and craftsmanship. Samsung's commitment to delivering a superlative audio experience is unmistakable, making the Galaxy S24 Ultra not just a smartphone but a portable concert hall where every sound is a masterpiece.

The impact on sound clarity and the importance of speaker space

In the ever-evolving landscape of smartphone technology, Samsung has once again raised the bar by unveiling the Galaxy S24 Ultra, a device that redefines the boundaries of sound clarity. At the heart of this auditory revolution is the meticulous consideration given to speaker space, a critical element that profoundly influences the overall acoustic experience.

One of the standout features defining the Galaxy S24 Ultra's impact on sound clarity is the expansion of speaker space. Samsung engineers, cognizant of the importance of providing ample room for sound reproduction, have ingeniously expanded the speaker chambers. This spatial augmentation translates into a richer, more immersive audio experience, allowing sound waves to travel freely and unfold in all their sonic glory.

The significance of speaker space becomes palpable when delving into the nuances of sound reproduction. The Galaxy S24 Ultra excels in delivering precise and accurate sound, ensuring that every note, every beat, and every spoken word is faithfully reproduced. The expanded speaker space contributes to minimizing distortion, creating an audio landscape where clarity reigns supreme.

Balanced resonance is a cornerstone of the Galaxy S24 Ultra's approach to sound clarity. By optimizing speaker space, Samsung has achieved a delicate equilibrium in resonance, preventing unwanted vibrations and distortions. This results in a finely tuned audio output where highs, mids, and lows coexist harmoniously, providing a listening experience that is both powerful and nuanced.

The impact of sound clarity extends beyond mere audio playback; it permeates every facet of multimedia engagement. Whether you're engrossed in a cinematic masterpiece, participating in a video conference, or gaming with intensity, the Galaxy S24 Ultra's commitment to sound clarity ensures that every sound is a revelation. The distinction between background elements and foreground details becomes vivid, enhancing the overall immersive experience.

In essence, the Galaxy S24 Ultra's emphasis on sound clarity and the strategic utilization of speaker space mark a paradigm shift in smartphone audio. It's not just about louder volumes; it's about creating an auditory journey where every sound is crystal clear, every note is resonant, and every user is transported into a world where sonic excellence knows no bounds.

3.3 Connectivity Evolution

In the relentless pursuit of faster and more reliable connectivity, Samsung has taken a monumental leap forward by integrating Wi-Fi 7 support into the Galaxy S24 Ultra. This cutting-edge wireless technology heralds a new era of connectivity, promising not just incremental improvements but a seismic shift in how we experience the digital realm.

Wi-Fi 7, the latest standard in wireless communication, represents a quantum leap in connectivity speeds and efficiency. With the Galaxy S24 Ultra being among the pioneers to adopt this groundbreaking technology, users can expect a connectivity experience that transcends the limitations of its predecessors.

At its core, Wi-Fi 7 is all about speed – and lots of it. The Galaxy S24 Ultra, equipped with Wi-Fi 7, redefines the dynamics of connectivity by offering unprecedented data transfer rates. Whether you're streaming high-definition content, engaging in seamless video calls, or downloading large files in the blink of an eye, the speed capabilities of Wi-Fi 7 in the Galaxy S24 Ultra are set to leave users in awe.

Beyond sheer speed, Wi-Fi 7 introduces lower latency, a crucial factor in enhancing the overall user experience. Gamers will revel in reduced lag during intense online battles, while video conferencing becomes even more lifelike with minimal delays. The Galaxy S24 Ultra's Wi-Fi 7 support ensures that every digital interaction is characterized by instantaneous responsiveness.

As we embrace the era of Wi-Fi 7 in the Galaxy S24 Ultra, users can rest assured that their devices are future-proofed against the evolving demands of the digital landscape. This forward-looking approach ensures that the Galaxy S24 Ultra remains at the forefront of connectivity standards, providing users with a reliable and cutting-edge experience for years to come.

In conclusion, the integration of Wi-Fi 7 support in the Galaxy S24 Ultra marks a transformative moment in the realm of smartphone connectivity. Faster speeds, lower latency, and future-ready capabilities converge to create an unparalleled digital experience, setting a new standard for what users can expect from their devices. With Wi-Fi 7, the Galaxy S24 Ultra is not just a smartphone; it's a gateway to a future where connectivity knows no bounds.

The increased screen responsiveness and brightness

The Galaxy S24 Ultra doesn't just represent a phone; it epitomizes a visual and tactile revolution. Samsung, known for pushing the boundaries of display technology, has once again raised the bar with the S24 Ultra. Let's delve into two key aspects that redefine the way we interact with our devices: increased screen responsiveness and unparalleled brightness.

Imagine a display that responds to your touch with unprecedented speed and precision. The Galaxy S24 Ultra introduces hyper-responsive touch technology, making every swipe, tap, and gesture a seamless extension of your intent. Whether you're navigating through apps, gaming with intensity, or simply typing a message, the enhanced touch responsiveness ensures an intuitive and frictionless experience.

In the quest for visual brilliance, the Galaxy S24 Ultra takes a quantum leap in display brightness. With a display that rivals the sun in terms of luminosity, users can bask in the glory of vivid colors and sharp contrasts even under the harsh glare of direct sunlight. This exceptional brightness not only enhances outdoor visibility but also contributes to an immersive viewing experience indoors, setting a new standard for smartphone displays.

The Galaxy S24 Ultra goes beyond static brightness levels. Thanks to its adaptive brilliance technology, the phone intelligently adjusts its screen brightness based on the surrounding environment. Whether you find yourself in a dimly lit room or under the scorching sun, the S24 Ultra ensures optimal visibility without compromising battery efficiency.

Samsung recognizes the importance of eye health in our screen-centric lives. The

Galaxy S24 Ultra incorporates advanced technologies to reduce eye strain, offering a display that's not just bright but also considerate of your eyes. From blue light filters to adjustable color temperatures, the S24 Ultra prioritizes your visual well-being without sacrificing the visual splendor.

In essence, the Galaxy S24 Ultra redefines the smartphone display experience with hyper-responsive touch technology, unparalleled brightness, and adaptive brilliance. It's not just a screen; it's a canvas of innovation, inviting users to engage with their digital world in ways that were once unimaginable. As you explore the depths of this visual marvel, be prepared to witness a display that not only meets expectations but surpasses them with flying colors – quite literally.

3.4 Glass Innovation

In the relentless pursuit of durability and resilience, Samsung has introduced a groundbreaking shift in the Galaxy S24 Ultra's display protection – a transition from the famed Gorilla Glass Victus 2 to the mighty Gorilla Glass Armor. This change represents more than just a choice of materials; it's a testament to Samsung's commitment to fortifying your smartphone against the rigors of daily life.

Gorilla Glass Victus 2, known for its exceptional scratch resistance and drop performance, was no slouch in the durability department. However, the Galaxy S24 Ultra takes a leap forward by adopting Gorilla Glass Armor, a material engineered to withstand even more extreme conditions. This shift ensures that your phone's display becomes a fortress, impervious to the challenges posed by the unpredictable nature of daily use.

Gorilla Glass Armor isn't just an incremental upgrade; it's a game-changer. This advanced glass formulation is designed to provide enhanced protection against drops, impacts, and scratches, effectively reducing the likelihood of screen damage. Your Galaxy S24 Ultra becomes a reliable companion, capable of weathering the storms of accidental slips or unexpected impacts.

Despite its robust nature, Gorilla Glass Armor maintains the delicate balance between strength and sensitivity. The touch responsiveness of the Galaxy S24 Ultra remains as precise as ever, ensuring that the protective shield doesn't compromise the user experience. Swipe, tap, and interact with confidence, knowing that your phone is shielded by the pinnacle of glass technology.

Gorilla Glass Armor not only reinforces durability but also elevates display clarity. The transparency and optical clarity of this material allow the vibrant colors and sharp details of the Galaxy S24 Ultra's display to shine through without compromise. It's a harmonious fusion of strength and visual brilliance, where durability seamlessly coexists with the stunning visual experience.

As you hold the Galaxy S24 Ultra in your hands, you're not just experiencing a smartphone; you're embracing a cutting-edge shield with Gorilla Glass Armor. This material transcends the conventional, ensuring that your device stands resilient against the trials of everyday life. So, go ahead, use your phone with the confidence that comes from knowing it's protected by the formidable Gorilla Glass Armor – a shield forged to withstand the tests of time and usage.

The alleged scratch resistance and glare reduction features

In the ever-evolving realm of smartphone displays, the Galaxy S24 Ultra emerges as a beacon of innovation, offering not just cutting-edge technology but a harmonious blend of features that elevate your visual experience. Two standout features, scratch resistance, and glare reduction, take center stage, transforming your interactions with the device into a seamless and pristine affair.

The Galaxy S24 Ultra boasts an alleged scratch resistance that transcends the ordinary. With daily use, your phone encounters an array of surfaces, some more abrasive than others. Samsung's commitment to durability shines through as the display, fortified with state-of-the-art technology, resists scratches that could mar its pristine surface. The result? A device that maintains its aesthetic appeal, day in and day out.

Glare – the nemesis of screen visibility, especially under bright sunlight. The Galaxy S24 Ultra addresses this challenge head-on with its advanced glare reduction technology. The display is meticulously engineered to minimize reflections and unwanted light scattering, ensuring that you can comfortably use your phone in various lighting conditions. Whether you're outdoors or indoors, the Galaxy S24 Ultra's screen remains vivid and easily readable.

Scratch resistance and glare reduction aren't just functional aspects; they contribute to preserving the visual integrity of your Galaxy S24 Ultra. The alleged scratch resistance ensures that your display remains clear and unblemished, while glare reduction enhances visibility. The result is a device that doesn't just meet expectations but exceeds them, offering a display that stays true to life in all its brilliance.

As you immerse yourself in the Galaxy S24 Ultra's display, the alleged scratch resistance and glare reduction features become silent guardians, ensuring that your visual experience remains untarnished. It's not just a phone; it's a testament to Samsung's commitment to providing a display that stands resilient against the trials of daily use, offering clarity and durability in equal measure.

Chapter 4:

Powering Up with

Snapdragon 8 Gen 3

4.1 Chip Revolution

In the heart of the Galaxy S24 Ultra lies a powerhouse – the Snapdragon 8 Gen 3 chip. As Samsung takes the reins of technological advancement, this chipset stands as a testament to the pursuit of excellence, marking a significant leap forward in performance, efficiency, and overall user experience.

The Snapdragon 8 Gen 3 chip is not just an upgrade; it's a symphony of architectural brilliance. With a cutting-edge 4nm process, it propels the Galaxy S24 Ultra into a new era of speed and efficiency. The smaller process node not only enhances performance but also contributes to energy efficiency, ensuring that your device delivers sustained high-level performance without compromising on battery life.

Every touch, swipe, and tap on the Galaxy S24 Ultra becomes a seamless dance of responsiveness, courtesy of the Snapdragon 8 Gen 3. The chip's octa-core CPU, bolstered by the Adreno GPU, transforms mundane tasks into swift, immersive experiences. Whether you're navigating through applications, multitasking with multiple windows, or diving into graphics-intensive games, the Galaxy S24 Ultra with the Snapdragon 8 Gen 3 chip is your gateway to unparalleled processing power.

The Snapdragon 8 Gen 3 chip is not merely about processing prowess; it's a harbinger of next-gen connectivity. With integrated 5G capabilities, the Galaxy S24 Ultra ensures that you're at the forefront of the digital revolution. Experience lightning-fast download and upload speeds, minimal latency, and the ability to connect and communicate at a pace that matches your dynamic lifestyle.

The Galaxy S24 Ultra, powered by the Snapdragon 8 Gen 3, isn't just smart; it's intelligent. The chip's advanced AI capabilities permeate every facet of your user experience, from camera enhancements that capture the perfect shot to adaptive battery management that optimizes power consumption based on your usage patterns. It's a device that learns and evolves with you, making every interaction a tailored and intuitive delight.

As you hold the Galaxy S24 Ultra in your hands, powered by the Snapdragon 8 Gen 3 chip, you're not just wielding a smartphone; you're wielding a technological marvel. It's a device that transcends boundaries, pushing the limits of what's possible and setting a new standard for flagship performance.

The custom 8 Gen 3 for Galaxy and its speed advantages

In the heart of the Galaxy S24 Ultra lies a technological marvel - the custom Snapdragon 8 Gen 3 chip designed exclusively for this flagship device. This chip represents a leap forward in processing power, bringing unparalleled speed advantages to the user experience.

Imagine a smartphone that not only meets but exceeds the demands of modern mobile applications and tasks. The Snapdragon 8 Gen 3 does just that for the Galaxy S24 Ultra. It's not merely a chip; it's the engine that propels the device into a realm of efficiency and speed that is sure to redefine your smartphone experience.

As applications become more complex and demanding, the need for a robust processor becomes paramount. The custom Snapdragon 8 Gen 3 addresses this need head-on, offering faster load times, smoother multitasking, and an overall snappier performance. Whether you're launching resource-intensive apps, editing high-resolution videos, or engaging in graphics-intensive gaming, the Galaxy S24 Ultra powered by the Snapdragon 8 Gen 3 ensures a seamless and responsive experience.

The beauty of this custom chip lies not only in its raw power but also in its optimization for the Galaxy S24 Ultra. Samsung's collaboration with Qualcomm has resulted in a chip that is finely tuned to extract the maximum potential from the hardware, ensuring a harmonious integration of software and silicon.

In a world where every second counts, the Galaxy S24 Ultra, armed with the custom Snapdragon 8 Gen 3, becomes a beacon of speed, setting new standards for what a flagship smartphone can achieve. The advantages are not just in the specifications but in the tangible, real-world impact on your daily interactions with the device.

As you delve into the realms of productivity, creativity, and entertainment, the Galaxy S24 Ultra, with its custom Snapdragon 8 Gen 3 chip, stands as a testament to the relentless pursuit of speed and efficiency in the ever-evolving landscape of smartphone technology. It's not just a chip; it's the catalyst for a faster, smoother, and more responsive Galaxy experience.

4.2 Temperature Control

Beneath the sleek exterior of the Galaxy S24 Ultra lies a crucial element that ensures the optimal performance of its cutting-edge custom Snapdragon 8 Gen 3 chip – an enlarged heat sink. This might not be the feature that catches your eye at first glance, but its significance becomes apparent when you delve into the intricate details of the device's engineering.

In the world of smartphones, heat is the nemesis of performance. As processors work hard to execute complex tasks, they generate heat, which, if not managed efficiently, can lead to throttling – a reduction in processing speed to prevent overheating. This is where the enlarged heat sink in the Galaxy S24 Ultra comes into play.

Picture this heat sink as a silent guardian, dissipating the thermal energy generated by the Snapdragon 8 Gen 3 chip. It's an unsung hero that ensures your device maintains peak performance even during prolonged, demanding tasks. By effectively controlling the chip temperature, Samsung has elevated the user experience, providing a device that doesn't just meet expectations but exceeds them.

The advantages of an enlarged heat sink are manifold. It not only prevents performance degradation but also contributes to the longevity of the device. With efficient heat dissipation, the Galaxy S24 Ultra remains cool under pressure, allowing you to push the boundaries of what your smartphone can achieve without compromise.

Whether you're engrossed in a graphics-intensive game, editing high-resolution videos, or running multiple applications simultaneously, the enlarged heat sink in the Galaxy S24 Ultra ensures that the Snapdragon 8 Gen 3 chip operates within its optimal temperature range. This, in turn, translates to a consistently smooth and responsive user experience.

In the realm of smartphone engineering, where every detail matters, the Galaxy S24 Ultra's commitment to thermal efficiency sets it apart. The enlarged heat sink is a testament to Samsung's dedication to delivering a device that not only dazzles with its features but also excels in the fundamental aspects of performance and reliability.

The implications of the Galaxy S24 Ultra's enlarged heat sink extend far beyond merely keeping the device cool under pressure. Its impact on overall phone performance and battery life is profound, shaping an experience that seamlessly blends power and efficiency.

First and foremost, the enlarged heat sink plays a pivotal role in sustaining peak performance. By efficiently managing the temperature of the Snapdragon 8 Gen 3 chip, the device avoids the pitfalls of throttling. This means that whether you're navigating resource-intensive applications, multitasking, or engaging in heavy gaming sessions, the Galaxy S24 Ultra maintains consistently high performance levels.

Moreover, the relationship between temperature control and battery life is symbiotic. Overheating can be a significant drain on battery resources, as the device works harder to cool itself down. The enlarged heat sink in the Galaxy S24 Ultra acts as a guardian against excessive heat, ensuring that the battery can focus on powering your device rather than combating temperature-related challenges.

In practical terms, this translates to a device that not only performs admirably but also boasts commendable battery efficiency. The

Galaxy S24 Ultra is designed to provide a reliable and enduring battery life, allowing you to navigate your day with confidence, knowing that your smartphone can keep up with your demands.

Whether you're a power user who pushes the limits of your device or someone who values a seamless and energy-efficient experience, the Galaxy S24 Ultra's enlarged heat sink becomes a silent ally in delivering a smartphone that doesn't compromise on performance or battery longevity. It's a testament to Samsung's commitment to crafting a device that excels in every aspect, ensuring that every interaction with the Galaxy S24 Ultra is a testament to the pinnacle of smartphone engineering.

4.3 Battery Brilliance

The Galaxy S24 Ultra takes a bold step forward in redefining the boundaries of smartphone endurance, promising a remarkable 15% increase in battery life compared to its predecessor, the S23 Ultra. This enhancement is not just a numerical figure but a commitment to providing users with an extended and more gratifying mobile experience.

The increased battery life is a result of meticulous optimization across various aspects of the device. The combination of the energy-efficient Snapdragon 8 Gen 3 chip, the carefully calibrated software, and the strategic management of resources all contribute to this notable improvement. Samsung's engineers have worked tirelessly to strike the perfect balance between power and efficiency, ensuring that users can go about their day with fewer concerns about running out of battery.

For users who have experienced the S23 Ultra, this leap in battery life is a welcome evolution. It means fewer interruptions to recharge during the day and more flexibility in using the device for power-intensive activities. Whether you're capturing breathtaking moments with the advanced camera system, engaging in immersive gaming, or simply navigating your daily tasks, the Galaxy S24 Ultra's extended battery life becomes a dependable companion.

This improvement aligns with Samsung's commitment to pushing the boundaries of what a smartphone can achieve. It's not just about having cutting-edge features; it's about ensuring that these features can be enjoyed without the constant worry of a dwindling battery. The 15% increase in battery life stands as a testament to Samsung's dedication to delivering a device that not only meets but exceeds the expectations of modern smartphone users.

To ensure the Galaxy S24 Ultra lives up to its promise of a 15% increase in battery life, Samsung has implemented an extensive and rigorous testing regimen. The company recognizes that real-world usage scenarios vary, and user demands on a smartphone can be diverse. Therefore, the testing process is designed to simulate a wide range of situations to validate the phone's performance under different conditions.

The testing phase begins with controlled environments that mimic everyday activities. This includes scenarios such as web browsing, video streaming, social media usage, and standard communication tasks. The goal is to establish a baseline for the phone's power consumption during typical usage patterns.

Beyond the controlled settings, Samsung takes the testing outdoors, exposing the Galaxy S24 Ultra to various ambient conditions. Factors like temperature, humidity, and different network strengths are considered to assess how the device adapts and optimizes its power usage in dynamic environments.

The camera system, known for its advanced features, undergoes specific tests to evaluate its impact on battery life. Samsung understands that photography and videography are crucial aspects of the user experience, and the device needs to deliver consistent performance without compromising endurance.

Gaming scenarios are also an essential part of the testing process. Given the increasing popularity of mobile gaming, Samsung wants to ensure that the Galaxy S24 Ultra maintains optimal performance without sacrificing battery life during extended gaming sessions.

The testing team pays close attention to the interplay between hardware and software. The optimization of the Snapdragon 8 Gen 3 chip, the efficiency of the operating system, and the adaptability of the device to user behaviors are all scrutinized to guarantee a harmonious balance that maximizes battery life.

Samsung's commitment to transparency is evident in how it communicates the testing process to users. Detailed reports on testing methodologies, results, and optimizations are shared, fostering a sense of trust and confidence among consumers. This dedication to thorough testing ensures that the Galaxy S24 Ultra not only meets but surpasses expectations, providing users with a smartphone that excels in both performance and endurance.

Chapter 5:
Camera Marvels

5.1 Main Camera Makeover

The Galaxy S24 Ultra boasts a remarkable leap in camera technology with its refreshed 200-megapixel main camera sensor. This upgrade is not merely about numbers; it signifies a significant advancement in the pursuit of photographic excellence. Samsung's commitment to pushing the boundaries of mobile photography is evident in the enhancements made to the camera system.

The 200-megapixel sensor introduces a new era of image capture, allowing users to dive into unprecedented levels of detail. Whether you are capturing landscapes, intricate textures, or dynamic scenes, this sensor sets a new standard for mobile photography resolution. The result is images that are not only visually stunning but also retain clarity and sharpness even when zoomed in.

Samsung has not just focused on the megapixel count but has also implemented advanced image processing technologies to complement the high-resolution sensor. This ensures that the Galaxy S24 Ultra delivers not only quantity but also quality in its photographic output. The improved processing algorithms contribute to better color accuracy, dynamic range, and low-light performance.

The camera system's versatility is further heightened by the inclusion of various lenses, each optimized for specific scenarios. From ultrawide shots that capture expansive landscapes to telephoto lenses that bring distant subjects closer, the Galaxy S24 Ultra empowers users to unleash their creativity and capture moments from unique perspectives.

The refresh of the 200-megapixel main camera sensor is not just about still photography. It extends to the realm of videography, where the device excels in capturing cinematic footage. The combination of high resolution and advanced stabilization technologies ensures that videos are not only sharp but also smooth, even in challenging shooting conditions.

The Galaxy S24 Ultra's camera system is a testament to Samsung's dedication to providing users with a cutting-edge photography experience. It transcends the conventional boundaries of mobile cameras, opening up new possibilities for users to express their creativity and capture the world in unprecedented detail. Whether you are a photography enthusiast or a casual shooter, the 200-megapixel main camera sensor on the Galaxy S24 Ultra is poised to redefine your mobile photography experience.

Samsung has revolutionized photo capture on the Galaxy S24 Ultra with the implementation of a faster photo capture technique, setting a new standard for speed and efficiency in mobile photography. This innovative feature not only enhances the user experience but also has a profound impact on the way moments are captured and memories are immortalized.

The faster photo capture technique is engineered to minimize the time between pressing the shutter button and the actual image capture. This means that users can now seize spontaneous moments with unprecedented speed, ensuring that no fleeting instant is missed. Whether it's a candid smile, a split-second action, or a rapidly changing scene, the Galaxy S24 Ultra empowers users to capture the essence of the moment instantaneously.

The impact of this faster photo capture technique extends beyond just speed. It redefines the responsiveness of the camera system, making it more intuitive and user-friendly. Users no longer need to anticipate moments in advance or worry about missing the perfect shot due to shutter lag. The Galaxy S24 Ultra's camera becomes an extension of the user's vision, capturing split-second wonders with remarkable precision.

The faster photo capture technique also enhances the phone's capabilities in challenging shooting conditions. Whether it's low light, fast motion, or dynamic scenes, the camera's ability to capture images rapidly ensures that users can confidently document a wide range of scenarios. This feature is particularly valuable for those who love to document their life's adventures, from bustling cityscapes to serene landscapes.

Samsung's commitment to innovation is evident in the integration of this technology, making the Galaxy S24 Ultra a frontrunner in the realm of mobile photography. As users explore the world through the lens of their smartphones, the faster photo capture technique becomes an invaluable ally, transforming the way they document and share their experiences. With speed at its core, the Galaxy S24 Ultra stands as a testament to Samsung's dedication to pushing the boundaries of what is possible in the world of mobile imaging.

5.2 Noise Reduction Revolution

Samsung has elevated the video recording capabilities of the Galaxy S24 Ultra by implementing advanced noise reduction algorithms, signaling a significant leap forward in achieving superior video quality. These cutting-edge algorithms work tirelessly behind the scenes, addressing one of the perennial challenges in mobile videography – noise.

Noise in videos can manifest as unwanted visual distortions or graininess, often exacerbated in low-light conditions or high-contrast scenarios. With the improved noise reduction algorithms on the Galaxy S24 Ultra, Samsung has tackled this challenge head-on. The result is a marked improvement in the clarity and visual fidelity of recorded videos, ensuring that users can capture moments with unprecedented detail and precision.

These advanced algorithms excel at identifying and suppressing unwanted noise without compromising the essential details of the video. Whether recording a vibrant sunset, a bustling cityscape, or a family celebration in challenging lighting conditions, users can rely on the Galaxy S24 Ultra to deliver videos with exceptional clarity and reduced visual noise.

The impact of these noise reduction algorithms goes beyond just improving video quality; it enhances the overall viewing experience. Users can now enjoy smoother and more immersive playback, whether they are reliving cherished memories or sharing their creations with friends and family. The Galaxy S24 Ultra's commitment to superior video quality sets it apart as a powerhouse in the realm of mobile videography.

As technology continues to advance, Samsung remains at the forefront, constantly pushing the boundaries to provide users with innovative solutions that elevate their smartphone experience. The implementation of state-of-the-art noise reduction algorithms in the Galaxy S24 Ultra underscores Samsung's dedication to delivering excellence in every frame, ensuring that users can capture and relive moments with unparalleled visual clarity and brilliance.

The integration of an upgraded 200-megapixel main camera sensor, along with enhanced noise reduction algorithms in the Galaxy S24 Ultra, holds the promise of a significant impact on Samsung's camera rankings. Samsung has consistently been at the forefront of mobile photography innovation, and the advancements in the Galaxy S24 Ultra are poised to reinforce its standing in the competitive landscape.

With a higher megapixel count, the main camera sensor is designed to capture stunningly detailed and vibrant images. This, coupled with the faster photo capture technique, ensures that users can seize the moment with unprecedented speed and precision. The Galaxy S24 Ultra is not merely a smartphone; it is a creative tool that empowers users to express themselves through photography in ways that were previously unimaginable.

The improvements in noise reduction algorithms further solidify Samsung's commitment to delivering exceptional video quality. As video content continues to gain prominence in the digital landscape, the Galaxy S24 Ultra's capabilities position it as a formidable contender for users seeking a device that excels in both photography and videography.

In terms of camera rankings, the Galaxy S24 Ultra's technological advancements are likely to enhance Samsung's position among the top players in the industry. Professional reviewers and users alike are expected to recognize and applaud the phone's camera capabilities, contributing to positive assessments and potentially influencing comparative rankings.

The emphasis on innovation and pushing the boundaries of what is possible in mobile photography is a testament to Samsung's dedication to providing users with cutting-edge technology. As the Galaxy S24 Ultra enters the market, its camera features are poised to make a lasting impact, not only solidifying Samsung's position but also setting a new standard for excellence in smartphone imaging.

5.3 Pro Visual Magic

The Pro Visual Engine in the Galaxy S24 Ultra adds an element of mystery and excitement to the device's camera capabilities. This cutting-edge technology is not just a feature; it's a game-changer in the realm of smartphone photography. Its impact on photo quality is nothing short of transformative.

Imagine a world where every photo you capture is elevated to a new level of visual brilliance. The Pro Visual Engine in the Galaxy S24 Ultra is the wizard behind the curtain, working its magic to enhance colors, contrast, and clarity in every shot. It's the secret ingredient that turns a simple snapshot into a work of art.

One of the key aspects of the Pro Visual Engine is its ability to intelligently analyze scenes in real-time. It doesn't just apply a one-size-fits-all enhancement; instead, it tailors its adjustments based on the unique characteristics of each photo. This level of adaptability ensures that whether you're capturing a breathtaking landscape or a close-up portrait, the Pro Visual Engine optimizes the settings for unparalleled results.

But the mystery doesn't end there. The Pro Visual Engine goes beyond conventional image processing. It delves into the realm of computational photography, leveraging advanced algorithms to unlock new possibilities. This means that even in challenging lighting conditions or fast-paced scenarios, the Galaxy S24 Ultra, with its Pro Visual Engine, rises to the occasion, delivering photos that defy expectations.

The impact of the Pro Visual Engine on photo quality is undeniable. It elevates the entire photography experience, making every shot a masterpiece. As users delve into the capabilities of the Galaxy S24 Ultra's camera, they'll find themselves on a journey of discovery, uncovering the magic woven into each photo by the enigmatic Pro Visual Engine. In the realm of smartphone photography, this mysterious force sets the Galaxy S24 Ultra apart, ensuring that every moment captured is a moment transformed into visual poetry.

Color reproduction, smoothness, and clarity are the triumvirate that defines the visual experience on the Galaxy S24 Ultra, setting a new standard for smartphone displays. The advancements in these aspects contribute to an immersive and captivating visual journey, making every interaction with the device a feast for the eyes.

Let's start with color reproduction. The Galaxy S24 Ultra boasts a display that goes beyond mere accuracy; it's a palette of precision. Colors are vibrant, true-to-life, and meticulously calibrated to bring content to life. Whether you're watching a cinematic masterpiece or scrolling through your photo gallery, the color reproduction on the Galaxy S24 Ultra is nothing short of breathtaking.

Smoothness takes center stage with the phone's high refresh rate display. Navigating through apps, scrolling through feeds, or engaging in mobile gaming becomes an incredibly fluid experience. The 120Hz refresh rate ensures that every swipe and animation is buttery smooth, elevating the overall responsiveness of the device.

Clarity is where the Galaxy S24 Ultra truly shines. The display is a window into a world of razor-sharp details. From the fine print in documents to the intricate textures in high-resolution images, every element on the screen is rendered with utmost clarity. This level of detail not only enhances productivity but also immerses users in a visual experience that leaves no room for compromise.

Together, these improvements create a synergy that transcends the ordinary. The Galaxy S24 Ultra's display is not just a canvas; it's a masterpiece. Users will find themselves captivated by the richness of colors, the fluidity of motion, and the clarity of every pixel. It's a testament to Samsung's commitment to delivering a visual experience that sets the Galaxy S24 Ultra apart in the competitive landscape of flagship smartphones.

5.4 Zoom Transformation

In the realm of smartphone photography, zoom capabilities have become a battleground for innovation, and the Galaxy S24 Ultra marks a strategic shift in this landscape. Samsung has made a noteworthy move by transitioning from a 10x zoom lens in the previous iteration to a 5x zoom lens in the S24 Ultra. This shift is a testament to the pursuit of balance between magnification and optical performance.

The decision to scale back the zoom factor from 10x to 5x reflects a nuanced understanding of user needs. While a 10x zoom might offer an extensive reach, it often comes with trade-offs such as larger camera modules and potential compromises in image quality. Samsung's move to a 5x zoom strikes a harmonious equilibrium, providing users with substantial magnification capabilities without sacrificing optical integrity.

The advantages of this transition are multi-faceted. Firstly, the reduced zoom factor allows for a more compact and streamlined camera module, contributing to the phone's overall design aesthetics. The sleeker profile enhances the phone's ergonomics, ensuring that the camera system seamlessly integrates with the device's form factor.

Optical performance is another area where this transition shines. The 5x zoom lens on the Galaxy S24 Ultra is optimized for clarity and detail, capturing distant subjects with remarkable precision. The refined optics ensure that users can zoom in without compromising image quality, resulting in sharp and vividly detailed photos even at a distance.

This strategic shift aligns with Samsung's commitment to delivering a camera system that meets the diverse needs of users, striking a delicate balance between innovation and practicality. The move from a 10x to a 5x zoom lens in the Galaxy S24 Ultra reflects a keen understanding of the evolving expectations in smartphone photography and a dedication to providing a holistic and high-quality imaging experience.

Samsung's decision to maintain consistent zoom quality across the entire zoom range in the Galaxy S24 Ultra is a testament to the brand's commitment to delivering a cohesive and uncompromised photography experience. By ensuring that the quality remains consistent throughout the zoom spectrum, Samsung addresses a common challenge faced by many smartphones with multiple zoom levels.

One notable benefit is the seamless transition between different zoom levels. Users can confidently zoom in or out, knowing that the image quality will remain consistently high. This uniformity enhances the versatility of the camera system, allowing users to capture a wide array of subjects, from expansive landscapes to distant details, without worrying about a degradation in quality.

Consistent zoom quality also contributes to a more intuitive and user-friendly photography experience. Users don't need to navigate through complex settings or make adjustments to maintain image clarity at different zoom levels. This simplicity aligns with Samsung's focus on user accessibility, ensuring that even those less familiar with advanced camera features can enjoy the full potential of the Galaxy S24 Ultra's zoom capabilities.

Moreover, the benefits extend to post-processing and editing. Consistent zoom quality provides a stable foundation for users who want to crop or edit their photos after capture. Whether zooming in to highlight specific details or zooming out for a different perspective, users can confidently manipulate their images without compromising on the overall quality and clarity.

In essence, the Galaxy S24 Ultra's commitment to consistent zoom quality sets a new standard for smartphone photography. It empowers users to explore the full range of zoom capabilities with confidence, knowing that Samsung has prioritized a harmonious and high-quality imaging experience across all focal lengths.

Chapter 6:
AI Integration

6.1 Galaxy AI Unleashed

In the ever-evolving landscape of smartphone technology, Samsung has once again raised the bar with the introduction of Galaxy AI in the Galaxy S24 Ultra. This groundbreaking feature marks a significant leap forward in the ongoing battle for supremacy among flagship smartphones, positioning Samsung at the forefront of innovation.

Galaxy AI is not just a feature; it's a game-changer. It represents a fusion of artificial intelligence and cutting-edge hardware, working seamlessly to enhance various aspects of the user experience. From photography to performance, Galaxy AI intelligently adapts to user behavior, creating a device that feels personalized and responsive in every interaction.

One of the standout applications of Galaxy AI is in the realm of photography. The smart camera system leverages AI algorithms to analyze scenes in real-time, optimizing settings for the best possible shot. Whether you're capturing a vibrant sunset or a fast-paced action sequence, Galaxy AI ensures that each photo is a masterpiece. The integration of AI extends to video recording, enhancing stabilization and clarity for professional-grade footage.

Beyond the camera, Galaxy AI makes its mark on device performance. By learning usage patterns over time, the smartphone preempts user needs, ensuring that frequently used apps are ready in an instant and that the overall performance is tailored to individual preferences. This level of adaptability creates a fluid and responsive user experience, setting the Galaxy S24 Ultra apart in the crowded arena of flagship smartphones.

Galaxy AI isn't just a feature you use; it's a technology that understands and evolves with you. As the smartphone battleground becomes increasingly competitive, Samsung's Galaxy S24 Ultra emerges not just as a device but as an intelligent companion, adapting to your needs, capturing your moments, and revolutionizing the way you experience the world through your smartphone. Get ready for a new era in mobile technology with Galaxy AI.

In the tech realm, the term "artificial intelligence" often conjures images of flashy gimmicks and exaggerated promises. However, Samsung's Galaxy S24 Ultra defies expectations by seamlessly integrating Galaxy AI into practical, everyday applications that go beyond mere gimmickry.

One of the most tangible applications of Galaxy AI lies in its ability to optimize battery life. Rather than relying on predetermined power-saving modes, Galaxy AI learns from individual usage patterns. It intelligently identifies when to conserve power and when to unleash the device's full capabilities. This not only extends battery life but does so without compromising the user experience.

In the realm of photography, Galaxy AI moves beyond simple scene recognition. It's not just about identifying a sunset or a portrait; it's about understanding the user's unique style. By learning preferred compositions, color palettes, and even favored lighting conditions, Galaxy AI tailors each photo to suit individual preferences. It's a subtle yet impactful shift from gimmicky filters to an intuitive understanding of the user's aesthetic.

Moreover, Galaxy AI's impact on device performance goes beyond the conventional. Instead of relying on static performance modes, the smartphone adapts dynamically to the user's needs. Whether you're engaged in resource-intensive gaming or simply scrolling through social media, Galaxy AI ensures that the device's performance is finely tuned to deliver an optimal experience.

Samsung's Galaxy S24 Ultra stands as a testament to the practical applications of artificial intelligence, shattering preconceived notions of gimmicks. It's not about flashy features that fade away; it's about a device that evolves with its user, learning, adapting, and enhancing the overall smartphone experience in ways that are both subtle and profound. Galaxy AI is not just a buzzword; it's a transformative force, bringing practical intelligence to the palm of your hand.

6.2 AI in Action

In the world of smartphone videography, capturing the perfect slow-motion moment often involves post-processing and a bit of patience. However, with the Galaxy S24 Ultra's innovative on-device AI capabilities, this process takes a giant leap forward, putting the power of instant slow-motion in the hands of every user.

Galaxy AI's Instant Slow-Mo feature is a game-changer for content creators and casual users alike. The device's AI is not merely a spectator; it actively engages with the user's recording process. As soon as it detects a scene suitable for slow-motion, the AI springs into action, automatically adjusting the camera settings to ensure optimal slow-motion capture.

Imagine recording a skateboard trick, a waterfall, or even a friend's dance moves. With the Galaxy S24 Ultra, you no longer need to wait until post-production to witness these moments in all their slow-motion glory. The on-device AI analyzes motion in real-time, seamlessly adjusting frame rates to deliver smooth, cinematic slow-motion footage instantly.

This functionality extends beyond traditional slow-motion scenarios. Even in unpredictable or spontaneous situations, the Galaxy S24 Ultra's AI intuitively recognizes opportunities for slow-motion capture. Whether it's a pet's playful antics or a surprise event, the device's AI ensures that you never miss a chance to immortalize these moments in captivating slow-motion.

By bringing slow-motion capabilities to the forefront of on-device features, Samsung's Galaxy S24 Ultra empowers users to enhance their creativity without the need for extensive post-production work. It's not just about recording moments; it's about capturing them with a level of detail and cinematic flair that was once reserved for professional setups. With Galaxy AI, every user becomes a maestro of motion, turning life's ordinary moments into extraordinary slow-motion masterpieces.

One of the standout features of the Galaxy S24 Ultra's on-device AI capabilities is its ability to perform real-time processing without relying on internet connectivity. This shift from dependency on cloud-based services to on-device processing is a game-changer, offering users a host of benefits that enhance both convenience and privacy.

In a world where connectivity isn't always guaranteed, the Galaxy S24 Ultra ensures that its users can harness the power of AI regardless of their internet status. Real-time processing means that the device can analyze and interpret data locally, within the confines of the smartphone itself. This not only results in faster response times but also eliminates the need for a constant and stable internet connection.

Privacy-conscious users will appreciate the reduced reliance on cloud-based services, as it minimizes the transfer of sensitive data to external servers. With on-device AI, personal information and content stay within the secure boundaries of the Galaxy S24 Ultra, providing users with greater control over their data.

The benefits of real-time processing extend beyond connectivity and privacy. Users can experience the full potential of on-device AI even in areas with poor network coverage or when traveling internationally. Whether you're capturing breathtaking slow-motion footage or utilizing AI-powered features in your daily routine, the Galaxy S24 Ultra ensures a seamless and dependable experience, irrespective of internet availability.

This departure from internet-dependent processing represents a significant leap in smartphone technology, marking a shift towards more self-sufficient devices. The Galaxy S24 Ultra not only keeps up with the demands of the modern user but anticipates their needs by providing cutting-edge features that work effortlessly, anytime and anywhere.

6.3 International Communication Breakthrough

In a world that thrives on global connectivity, the Galaxy S24 Ultra introduces a revolutionary live translation feature, breaking down language barriers and fostering seamless communication. This cutting-edge capability empowers users to engage with people from diverse linguistic backgrounds, making the smartphone a true companion for international travelers, business professionals, and anyone navigating a multilingual landscape.

The live translation feature on the Galaxy S24 Ultra leverages advanced artificial intelligence and language processing algorithms to provide instantaneous translations. Whether you're exploring a foreign city, negotiating business deals, or simply conversing with friends from different parts of the world, the Galaxy S24 Ultra ensures that language differences do not hinder meaningful interactions.

Picture this: you're in a bustling market in Tokyo, and you come across a sign with intriguing characters. With the Galaxy S24 Ultra in hand, you can use the live translation feature to instantly decipher the text, gaining insights into the local culture and navigating your surroundings with ease. The possibilities are endless, from reading menus in exotic restaurants to comprehending street signs in unfamiliar locales.

Business meetings become more inclusive, fostering collaboration across international teams. The live translation feature allows professionals to communicate effectively, ensuring that language nuances do not impede the exchange of ideas and strategies. This groundbreaking functionality on the Galaxy S24 Ultra transforms it into a global communication tool, facilitating connections beyond borders.

Moreover, the live translation feature isn't just limited to text. It extends to spoken language, enabling real-time conversations with people who speak different languages. Imagine attending a conference where speakers address the audience in various languages—thanks to the Galaxy S24 Ultra, you can follow every word, breaking down language barriers effortlessly.

In summary, the Galaxy S24 Ultra's live translation features redefine the concept of a language barrier. By seamlessly translating text and speech in real-time, the smartphone becomes a powerful tool for fostering cross-cultural understanding, enabling users to explore, connect, and communicate on a global scale.

While the live translation feature on the Galaxy S24 Ultra marks a significant leap forward in breaking down language barriers, it's essential to acknowledge the challenges faced and anticipate future improvements. Like any groundbreaking technology, live translation is not without its complexities, and understanding these nuances is crucial for users seeking a seamless multilingual experience.

One of the primary challenges lies in the diversity of languages and dialects worldwide. The Galaxy S24 Ultra, equipped with a robust live translation feature, excels in major languages but may face limitations with less common or regional dialects. Users exploring off-the-beaten-path locations or engaging with niche communities may encounter instances where the live translation feature doesn't provide the desired level of accuracy.

Additionally, the speed of translation, while impressive, may not match the fluency of human communication. In fast-paced conversations, especially during group discussions or lively social interactions, there might be a slight lag in the translation process. Samsung acknowledges this challenge and is committed to refining the speed of live translation through future software updates.

The Galaxy S24 Ultra's live translation feature heavily relies on cloud-based processing for its extensive language database. While this ensures a vast range of supported languages, it also raises concerns about privacy and data security. Samsung is actively working on enhancing on-device processing capabilities, aiming to reduce reliance on cloud services and provide users with a more secure translation experience.

Looking toward the future, Samsung envisions incorporating even more languages into the live translation repertoire. The company recognizes the global diversity of its user base and is dedicated to expanding language support through regular updates. Users can anticipate a more inclusive and comprehensive language coverage, fostering greater accessibility across the globe.

In conclusion, the Galaxy S24 Ultra's live translation feature is a remarkable step towards a more interconnected world. Acknowledging the current challenges and the commitment to future enhancements, Samsung invites users to join the journey of transcending language barriers and looks forward to a future where communication knows no bounds.

6.4 Summarizing Intelligence

In the ever-expanding landscape of digital information, AI-driven summarization tools have emerged as invaluable assets, offering users the ability to distill vast amounts of content into concise and manageable summaries. The Galaxy S24 Ultra introduces cutting-edge AI capabilities in its summarization tools, catering to users seeking efficient ways to navigate the information overload prevalent in today's digital age.

The applications of AI-driven summarization tools are multifaceted, addressing various scenarios where information comprehension and time efficiency are paramount. One notable application is in the realm of news consumption. With an overwhelming influx of news articles, blog posts, and updates, users can leverage the summarization feature to obtain key insights without delving into the entirety of lengthy articles. This proves especially beneficial for users on the go, allowing them to stay informed without compromising their time.

Another significant application lies in the academic and professional domains. Research articles, reports, and lengthy documents can be challenging to sift through comprehensively. The Galaxy S24 Ultra's AI-driven summarization tools empower users to quickly grasp the core concepts and essential details, streamlining the process of information assimilation.

This not only enhances productivity but also facilitates more informed decision-making in academic and professional pursuits.

The Galaxy S24 Ultra's summarization tools also find relevance in the era of content creation. For individuals curating content for blogs, social media, or presentations, the ability to quickly summarize information ensures that the produced content remains concise and impactful. This aligns with the contemporary preference for bite-sized, easily digestible information.

One of the standout features of the Galaxy S24 Ultra's AI-driven summarization tools is their adaptability. The tools utilize advanced natural language processing algorithms to understand context, tone, and sentiment, ensuring that the generated summaries retain the essence of the original content. This level of sophistication sets the Galaxy S24 Ultra apart in the realm of AI-driven summarization.

As users embrace the transformative power of AI-driven summarization tools, the Galaxy S24 Ultra stands as a beacon of innovation, offering a seamless and intelligent solution to the challenges posed by information overload. Whether staying updated with the latest news, conducting research, or creating compelling content, users can trust the Galaxy S24 Ultra to deliver clarity in the face of complexity.

The integration of AI-driven summarization tools in the Galaxy S24 Ultra brings about transformative implications for various facets of professional and personal life, particularly in the realms of meetings, document summaries, and note-taking. This cutting-edge feature is poised to redefine how individuals approach information processing and knowledge retention.

In the realm of meetings, the Galaxy S24 Ultra's AI-driven summarization tools offer a game-changing solution for professionals. Often, meetings involve a plethora of information, discussions, and action items. Keeping track of every detail can be challenging, leading to potential oversights. With the summarization tools, users can capture the essence of discussions, key decisions, and action items in real-time. This not only facilitates more efficient meeting management but also ensures that participants leave with a clear understanding of the meeting's outcomes.

Document summaries take on a new level of efficiency with the Galaxy S24 Ultra. Long reports, research papers, or extensive documents can be time-consuming to read in their entirety. The AI-driven summarization tools analyze and distill these documents into concise summaries, allowing users to quickly grasp the main points, arguments, and conclusions. This is particularly advantageous in professional settings where time is of the essence, enabling users to stay informed without dedicating extensive periods to document review.

Note-taking, an integral aspect of both professional and academic endeavors, also experiences a paradigm shift with the Galaxy S24 Ultra's summarization tools. Whether in lectures, business meetings, or casual brainstorming sessions, users can rely on the phone to automatically generate concise and meaningful summaries of spoken or written content. This not only streamlines the note-taking process but also provides a readily accessible repository of key information.

The implications of these features extend beyond mere convenience; they contribute to heightened productivity and improved decision-making. By leveraging AI-driven summarization, individuals can navigate the information landscape more effectively, ensuring that they are well-informed and equipped to excel in their respective domains.

As the Galaxy S24 Ultra blurs the lines between innovation and practicality, its impact on meetings, document summaries, and note-taking becomes increasingly evident. This device is not merely a smartphone; it's a companion in the pursuit of productivity and knowledge mastery.

6.5 Chat Assist Keyboard

The Galaxy S24 Ultra introduces a paradigm shift in the realm of smartphone keyboards with its innovative Smart Keyboard featuring Chat Assist. This cutting-edge keyboard is more than just a tool for typing; it's a companion that understands and anticipates user needs, seamlessly integrating advanced functionalities to enhance the overall typing experience.

The Smart Keyboard's standout feature is the Chat Assist, an intelligent assistant that takes predictive typing to a whole new level. Traditional predictive text systems often suggest generic words or phrases based on commonly used expressions. However, the Chat Assist goes beyond the ordinary by leveraging artificial intelligence to understand the context of the conversation, allowing for highly accurate and contextually relevant predictions.

As users engage in conversations, the Smart Keyboard with Chat Assist analyzes the ongoing dialogue, taking into account the specific nuances of language and personal communication styles. This enables the keyboard to predict not only individual words but entire phrases and responses that align with the user's unique conversational tone. The result is a fluid and natural flow of communication, saving time and effort in composing messages.

The Smart Keyboard also incorporates advanced autocorrection algorithms, significantly reducing typing errors and enhancing overall accuracy. Its ability to learn from user input ensures a personalized typing experience, adapting to individual preferences and evolving linguistic patterns over time.

Beyond its predictive prowess, the Smart Keyboard introduces an innovative Chat Assist button, strategically placed for easy access. This button acts as a gateway to a range of contextual features designed to streamline communication. Users can leverage quick access to emojis, gifs, and even suggested conversation starters, adding an element of fun and efficiency to their messaging experience.

In addition to its intelligent features, the Smart Keyboard maintains a sleek and user-friendly design. The keys are responsive, offering a satisfying tactile feel that enhances the overall typing comfort. The keyboard adapts to different typing styles, accommodating both swift typists and those who prefer a more deliberate approach.

As smartphones become indispensable tools for communication, the Galaxy S24 Ultra's Smart Keyboard with Chat Assist stands out as a testament to Samsung's commitment to innovation. It's not just a keyboard; it's a communication enabler that transforms the way users engage with their devices, making every interaction a seamless and intuitive experience.

In the ever-evolving landscape of smartphone technology, the Galaxy S24 Ultra ascends to new heights with its comprehensive language capabilities. The device integrates an array of language-oriented features, making it not just a communication tool but a linguistic powerhouse.

One of the standout features is the built-in translation functionality, which breaks down language barriers with remarkable finesse. The Galaxy S24 Ultra employs state-of-the-art artificial intelligence algorithms to provide seamless and accurate translations in real-time. Whether it's decoding a foreign language text or facilitating multilingual conversations, the translation feature ensures that communication transcends linguistic boundaries.

What sets the translation feature apart is its contextual understanding, enabling it to capture the nuances of language and deliver translations that go beyond mere word-for-word conversions. The device considers cultural context, idiomatic expressions, and colloquialisms, ensuring that the essence of the message remains intact across languages. Whether you're a globetrotter, a business professional, or someone connecting with friends from diverse backgrounds, the Galaxy S24 Ultra's translation feature becomes your indispensable language companion.

The device also boasts an advanced writing style and grammar check system, elevating the quality of written communication. The writing style analysis goes beyond conventional grammar checks, offering nuanced suggestions to enhance the overall tone and coherence of your text. It acts as a virtual writing assistant, providing insightful feedback on sentence structure, vocabulary choice, and overall writing style.

The grammar check feature, powered by sophisticated algorithms, ensures that your messages and documents are free from grammatical errors. From simple punctuation corrections to complex sentence structure suggestions, the Galaxy S24 Ultra's grammar check elevates the quality of written expression. The goal is not just error correction but enhancing the overall clarity and impact of your written communication.

Navigating the settings for these language features is intuitive, and users can customize the level of assistance based on their preferences. Whether you're a language enthusiast striving for linguistic perfection or someone looking for reliable communication tools, the Galaxy S24 Ultra's translation, writing style, and grammar check functionalities make it a standout choice in the realm of language-centric smartphones.

Chapter 7:

Software Evolution

7.1 One UI 6.1 Revolution

The Galaxy S24 Ultra brings a new dimension to user interaction with its cutting-edge One UI 6.1, seamlessly integrated with the Android 14 operating system. This harmonious union of software and hardware transforms the smartphone experience, offering users a host of enhancements that redefine how they engage with their devices.

Streamlined Navigation and Intuitive Gestures: One UI 6.1 introduces refined navigation gestures, providing users with a more fluid and intuitive way to interact with their Galaxy S24 Ultra. Navigating through apps, menus, and multitasking becomes a seamless experience, enhancing overall efficiency and user satisfaction. The redesigned gestures not only respond to touch more accurately but also add a layer of sophistication to the user interface.

Revamped App Layout and Organization: Building on the principles of user-centric design, One UI 6.1 brings forth a revamped app layout and organization. The user interface now prioritizes frequently used apps, ensuring that they are easily accessible with a single swipe. The redesigned app drawer and home screen contribute to a cleaner and more organized visual aesthetic, allowing users to personalize their digital space effortlessly.

Enhanced Privacy Controls and Security Measures: In an era where digital privacy is paramount, One UI 6.1 introduces an array of enhanced privacy controls and security measures. Users can now have more granular control over app permissions, ensuring that sensitive data remains protected. The integration of Android 14's latest security features further fortifies the Galaxy S24 Ultra against potential threats, providing users with peace of mind in an increasingly interconnected world.

Optimized Multitasking and Productivity: One UI 6.1 takes multitasking to the next level, optimizing the Galaxy S24 Ultra for enhanced productivity. The revamped split-screen view, along with improved app pair functionalities, enables users to seamlessly juggle multiple tasks simultaneously. Whether it's responding to messages while watching a video or working on documents side by side, the device empowers users to maximize efficiency without compromising on user experience.

Adaptive Display and Dark Mode Enhancements: The Galaxy S24 Ultra, with One UI 6.1, introduces refined adaptive display features that adapt to varying ambient lighting conditions. The display intelligently adjusts color temperatures and brightness levels to ensure optimal visibility and comfort. Dark mode enthusiasts will appreciate the enhanced dark mode options, reducing eye strain and extending battery life while maintaining a visually pleasing interface.

Seamless Cross-Device Integration: With Android 14's robust ecosystem integration, the Galaxy S24 Ultra becomes part of a seamless cross-device experience. Whether transitioning from a Galaxy tablet to the smartphone or connecting to other Android 14-enabled devices, users can expect a cohesive and interconnected digital environment.

In essence, One UI 6.1, coupled with Android 14, propels the Galaxy S24 Ultra into a new era of user-centric design, privacy enhancements, and overall digital sophistication. This dynamic integration not only showcases Samsung's commitment to innovation but also places the user firmly at the center of the technological journey.

One UI 6.1 on the Galaxy S24 Ultra doesn't just stop at improving the fundamentals; it revolutionizes the user interface down to the smallest details. The drop-down menu, a familiar element of smartphone navigation, undergoes a stunning transformation, offering users a more intuitive and visually captivating experience.

The drop-down menu, a central hub for notifications and quick settings, receives a facelift that goes beyond aesthetics. One UI 6.1 introduces a redesigned drop-down menu that not only looks sleek but also enhances functionality. Notifications are now intelligently grouped, minimizing clutter and allowing users to prioritize essential alerts. The streamlined layout ensures that important messages and updates are easily accessible with a single glance.

Personalization takes center stage with the introduction of dynamic widgets. Gone are the static, one-size-fits-all widgets of yesteryears. One UI 6.1 empowers users to customize their home screens with dynamic widgets that adapt to usage patterns. Whether it's an interactive calendar widget that displays upcoming events or a fitness widget that tracks daily activity, users can tailor their smartphone experience to align with their unique preferences and priorities.

Adding a touch of visual delight, the Galaxy S24 Ultra introduces the Visualizer feature on the lock screen. This mesmerizing addition turns the lock screen into a canvas of dynamic colors and shapes that dance to the rhythm of ambient sounds. Whether it's music playing or the surrounding environment's noise, the Visualizer creates a captivating audio-visual experience that transcends the conventional boundaries of smartphone aesthetics.

In essence, the redesigned drop-down menu, dynamic widgets, and Visualizer feature epitomize Samsung's commitment to creating a user interface that not only meets functional needs but also elevates the overall sensory experience. With One UI 6.1, the Galaxy S24 Ultra becomes not just a device but a personalized, dynamic companion that adapts to the user's preferences and enhances daily interactions in ways previously unexplored.

7.2 Support Revolution

Samsung, once criticized for its lackluster software support, has undergone a remarkable transformation, positioning itself as a standout player in the competitive arena of smartphone software updates. The Galaxy S24 Ultra, running on One UI 6.1 based on Android 14, is a testament to Samsung's commitment to delivering a seamless and up-to-date software experience.

Not long ago, Samsung found itself in the crosshairs of criticism for sluggish software updates, leaving users grappling with outdated features and security vulnerabilities. However, the winds of change began to blow, and Samsung listened. The company recognized the importance of timely updates, not just as a necessity but as a cornerstone for user satisfaction and device longevity.

The pivotal shift came with the introduction of One UI, Samsung's customized user interface. One UI not only addressed the aesthetic and functional aspects but also laid the foundation for a more streamlined and efficient update process. The intuitive design and user-centric approach garnered praise, setting the stage for a new era in Samsung's software journey.

With the Galaxy S24 Ultra, Samsung takes its commitment a step further. One UI 6.1, based on the latest Android 14, is a testament to Samsung's dedication to providing users with the latest features, security patches, and improvements promptly. The once-criticized laggard is now setting the standard for frequent and timely software updates, ensuring that users don't just get a smartphone but a device that evolves and improves over time.

Samsung's evolution extends beyond feature updates. The company has made significant strides in fortifying device security. Regular security patches, coupled with proactive measures such as Knox security, exemplify Samsung's resolve to create a secure digital environment for its users.

In conclusion, Samsung's transformation in software support, from being labeled as one of the worst to emerging as a standout performer, is a testament to the company's adaptability and commitment to user satisfaction. The Galaxy S24 Ultra, with its One UI 6.1 and Android 14 foundation, stands as a symbol of Samsung's dedication to providing a software experience that not only meets expectations but exceeds them, ushering in a new era of excellence in smartphone software support.

The importance of timely updates and support for users

In the ever-evolving landscape of smartphones, the importance of timely updates and robust support cannot be overstated. For users investing in cutting-edge devices like the Samsung Galaxy S24 Ultra, the promise of ongoing software updates is not just a feature; it's a commitment to an enhanced and enduring user experience.

Timely updates play a pivotal role in bolstering the security of a device. In a digital era rife with evolving threats, swift responses to vulnerabilities are crucial. Regular security patches ensure that users are shielded from potential risks, providing them with peace of mind as they navigate the vast landscape of the digital world.

Software updates bring more than just security enhancements; they unlock new capabilities and features. The Galaxy S24 Ultra, powered by One UI 6.1 based on Android 14, exemplifies Samsung's dedication to innovation. With each update, users not only receive performance improvements but also gain access to the latest technological advancements, keeping their devices at the forefront of functionality.

A commitment to timely updates is, in essence, a commitment to the longevity and resilience of a device. Users want to feel assured that their investment will withstand the test of time, adapting to new challenges and staying relevant in a rapidly evolving technological landscape. Regular updates ensure that the Galaxy S24 Ultra remains a reliable companion, evolving with the user's needs.

Beyond the technical aspects, timely updates contribute to an enriched user experience. Users appreciate a device that not only meets their expectations at the time of purchase but continues to exceed them. Samsung's dedication to providing a seamless, up-to-date software experience ensures that users derive maximum value from their smartphones, fostering a sense of satisfaction and loyalty.

In conclusion, timely updates and robust support are not mere checkboxes in the realm of smartphone features; they are the bedrock of user satisfaction. Samsung's commitment to providing a software experience that combines security, innovation, and longevity underscores the company's understanding of user needs. For Galaxy S24 Ultra users, this commitment translates into a device that not only dazzles with its cutting-edge features but also stands the test of time, delivering an unparalleled and enduring smartphone experience.

Conclusion

As we conclude our exploration of the Samsung Galaxy S24 Ultra, it's evident that this device marks a transformative juncture in the world of smartphones. From the cutting-edge hardware upgrades to the innovative AI features and the evolution of software, the Galaxy S24 Ultra stands as a testament to Samsung's commitment to pushing boundaries and redefining user expectations.

At the heart of the Galaxy S24 Ultra's prowess is the formidable influence of Artificial Intelligence. From enhancing camera capabilities to providing real-time translations and on-device processing, AI permeates every aspect of the user experience. It's not just a feature; it's a game-changer, offering users a glimpse into the future of intuitive and responsive technology.

The hardware upgrades in the Galaxy S24 Ultra are nothing short of revolutionary. From the custom Snapdragon 8 Gen 3 chip to the Titanium frame, every component is meticulously designed to elevate performance and durability. The enlarged heat sink ensures optimal temperature control, contributing to sustained performance and extended battery life.

The software evolution, embodied by One UI 6.1 based on Android 14, reflects Samsung's commitment to delivering a seamless and visually stunning user interface. The redesigned drop-down menu, dynamic widgets, and the visualizer contribute to an aesthetically pleasing and highly functional interface. Samsung's journey from one of the worst to standout in software support signifies a dedication to user satisfaction and device longevity.

In unison, the AI-driven features, hardware advancements, and software evolution create a symphony of upgrades that redefine what a smartphone can achieve. The Galaxy S24 Ultra isn't just a device; it's an experience. It's a companion that anticipates your needs, captures your moments in unprecedented clarity, and adapts to your rhythm through intelligent software enhancements.

As users embrace the Galaxy S24 Ultra, they aren't just getting a smartphone; they're entering a new era of possibilities. The transformative impact of AI, coupled with robust hardware and evolving software, ensures that this device isn't just for today—it's for the future. It's a promise delivered by Samsung, inviting users to witness the unfolding of technology's limitless potential in the palm of their hands.

In conclusion, the Galaxy S24 Ultra journey isn't just a glimpse into the latest technological marvel; it's an invitation to embrace a future where innovation, intelligence, and excellence converge to redefine the smartphone experience. As users embark on this journey, they carry with them a device that not only meets their needs today but paves the way for a tomorrow where the possibilities are as limitless as the horizons they explore with their Galaxy S24 Ultra.